Mixed root poems

Ezequiel Kratsman

Published by: Ezequiel David Publishing
ISBN: 978-1-954314-31-3
Second edition: 2025

Prologue

Every time I read a poem, I always have this thought on my mind: Every theme, every true event or mentioned feeling in a poem that's a handkerchief of word, small or long, but always with something to express, something to say and send a message or with a desire to express what he feels. And he does it by writing the words from the root of his heart and soul. Just like in boxing and mixed martial arts, in the art of writing, you can even express your biggest anger and hate without needing to hit. You can express your feelings after going through some kind of experience. And knowing myself and the experiences I went through, I can express how I feel when I remember those experiences through this mean, one of the best ways to do it. That's what I like about writing. When a person has an idea in his head, instead of saying it around, he can express through this art. Of course, you have to think the details and how to express them. When I started writing, that thought of me not making it to the top through writing started getting out my mind.

When I wrote this poetry book, I realized something every person can see: With every theme, a person can become more aware of his qualities as a person and what he can do to improve them. He can also discover his weaknesses in his personality and what he can do to eliminate them or improve. With every mentioned theme, I'm sure of sending a clear message to society and doing all the possible to make sure it's positive. I also want to entertain the reader with several ways of expression. All feelings will be expressed, including love. They can be expressed and shown with thousands of details. I hope you get entertained and enjoy them the way I did when I wrote them.

Index

It will always be like this   March 2020

The first time I saw you, we were two lost souls
that didn't know how far they could go.
You got really close to me with those sad wounds
that started healing with my comfort.
Let me comfort you
with all my adoration.
Let me treat you like a blessing
that has to be taken into consideration.

Trust me; tell me what I can do for you.
Tell me what details not to miss.
As long as you're close to me,
it will always be like this.
We were searching for our destiny like two pretty
condors
that were flying and were not done.
Every detail is so divine you can't let those sad pains
influence you because your life has just begun.

If you're by my side, the wounds
in your soul will disappear.
Your heart will feel loved again
and you'll a sunrise in it every year.
I can only give you love.
If you believe in me,
I'll always be there for you
like I know you'll be there for me.

You will not feel any fear.
There are no details I will not miss.
As long as you're close to me,
it will always be like this.

Heartbroken   March 2020

You may feel like a loser,
a thought that can be horrible.
But if you want to feel better
and cheer up, I'll be available.
You may think: "I want to go"
when you feel really lonely.
But many adore your personality,
so, you have to keep going firmly.

Those who think you should disappear
because you have some kind of issues
are ignorant because they don't know the real you
and they don't know your great virtues.
Although you feel alone in an arch,
a feeling that can even tempt you in a far land,
regardless of how deep that wound is, I want you
to think the following as I give you a hand:

When you have no one to give you comfort
and you want to feel lost in another world,
without any hope and in the ground,
you can count on me when you're hurt.
If you need to grief your pain,
I'll be available.
I can only love you and you can hug me
when you feel heartbroken.

There'll be always someone
who will make fun of you in any situation.
They'll do it to hurt your soul
and they'll do it with passion.
I want you to know I'll always defend you

and help get up the ground.
You can always believe in me
when you feel down.

I can't judge you for feeling hurt.
I can only love you and be available
and let you hug me
when you feel heartbroken.

With my head high   March 2020

I was hurt several times,
but my mind kept going every day and night.
I've been underappreciated, but I'll keep winning
every round, constantly battling with my head high.
People will keep making fun of me to try
to see my mental strength disappear,
but I'll keep believing in me,
succeeding year after year.

I've been hurt by people worse
than banging my head with a steering wheel.
I've gotten worse wounds that remain even in my bones,
but I'll move on with my great will.
Those who hurt me may be around somewhere,
trying to cross the line,
but I'll be fighting constantly, with my spirit telling me:
"Believe in yourself", to achieve the goals I have in
mind.

I'll keep battling ferociously, forgetting
about those who underestimated me, day and night
to achieve those goals, always willing to evolve
with my head high.

Ode to my heavy bag   March 2020

Although I don't use it with beauty,
I always hit it effectively.
It doesn't matter if years go by or I lose my voice,
I'll use the heavy bag constantly.
When I use the heavy hag, I unload
all the anger I have inside.
Although I don't have the best technique, I hit
with power and determination, and I feel better at night.

When I put the gloves on,
I get ready to unload all my fury
and I pretend I can break lot of steering wheels.
The rest is history.
I think it's a great workout
I can do with passion.
I love doing it because I do it at a great pace
without getting anyone's attention.

When I throw lefts, rights, and hooks, I throw them
with everything, making the sound of an earthquake.
When I finish a round,
I want to keep using it the same way.
I use it easily, hitting it
with the fury of a hurricane.
I'd rather use it than hit people around
and getting many complaints.

The heavy bag is the best workout.

I hit it with the ferocity of the legend called Hands of Stone.
I feel so much better
when the heavy bag session is done.

What was the authority doing?   March 2020

I can say almost half of my classmates
were a big torture.
Seeing them misbehaving was worse
than suffering a fissure.
They didn't want to stop
and they were the worst.
They did their bad mischiefs
with more energy than a racehorse.

They were a level of adversity you had
to overcome with patience, courage, and determination.
You didn't want to hate them, but they didn't give you
another choice in that situation.
During class, some of them talked
impulsively about everything.
It was like they couldn't reason.
I thought: What was the authority doing?

I didn't have anything in common with them.
They were truly impulsive and showed it with passion.
They showed their bad attitude
without caring about their education.
They were animals that seemed
to come out of a bush.
They were so bad they could cause a disease
you wanted to avoid in a rush.

It didn't matter if the accumulation
of complaints and reprimands were inexplicable.
They just didn't learn.
That's why reprimanding them was inevitable.

No disciplinary method could work with them.
They denied you a moment of peace for anything.
Everyone knew what was going on.
I wondered: What was the authority doing?

On the court   March 2020

It was in that place where I got a good image
and I even earned some fans.
I played every game with passion,
even when I had the ball in my hands.
This sport was part of great salvation
and many had a great experience in a day.
The crowd got excited
when I did a very good play.

I knew this sport was going to do
a good for me from the beginning.
When I played it, I felt like my Argentine
countryman and idol, who won everything.
I felt truly great for everything
I did on the court.
It made me have
the best mood in the world.

I was always ready to play,
knowing what I could do.
It was in that place where I could
really have peace; it's true.
I rarely slipped
when I was on the court.
But when I played, I did it
with all my heart and soul.

When the ball went in, it
made the fans get loud.
I was really happy when the game

really excited the crowd.
When I had the ball and shot it,
it was like practicing some type of art.
Although it wasn't always going to be exciting,
it brought peace to my heart.

The opponent's experience didn't matter.
It didn't matter if he was as big as a wall.
When the game started,
I was going to give it my all.
After the game was over,
we would give each other a handshake.
Whether it was a win or a loss,
we would get along at the end of the day.

Those were little moments of glory
when I played that great sport.
I wasn't the most skilled player,
but I had happy moments on the court.

That summer March 2020

It was supposed to be a good summer
after the last school day.
But a very sad experience
took it all away.
A girl who was a supposed friend
said some big lies about me.
It would've hurt my life
in a way no one could see.

Her effort to see me locked up
was in vain,
but it was monstrous.
and made my heart go through big pain.
The sadness and anger because of that moment
were thunderous.
During that summer, the bad feelings
due to those lies were disastrous.

The sadness and confusion were so big
that they got in my soul.
Nothing mattered to me.
I wanted to stop living in the world.
I was so hurt
I didn't want to get out of my home.
I felt really damaged and I thought
the pain was never going to be gone.

I felt bad with myself.
I felt complete internal devastation.
I didn't have any wish to talk to anyone.

I was completely in isolation.
Thankfully, I got some workout DVDs
so, I could work out at home and clear my mind.
Otherwise, the anger would've been deeper
and I needed that to spend my time.

My soul felt resentment and was
more shattered than an airplane.
During that summer, I felt
more isolated than a crane.

My brother from another mother   March 2020

I never had a fight with him.
He was impossible to hate.
I could always trust him
and I could talk to him any given day.
I knew he was never going to let me down.
If I needed some advice, he was there to help.
He always acted with intelligence.
We could talk about several subjects well.

If I needed someone to talk to,
he was there.
We could have long conversations;
it didn't matter when and where.
I always admired
his mental and physical agility.
He was an admirable person
and always showed his loyalty.

He's my brother from another mother.
I told him about my experiences.
He was someone you could count on
if you wanted to go long distances.
I would go to his house, or he would go to mine
to watch a fight or play chess.
He made me feel at home and I did the same thing
with him; those times were the best.

He's my brother from another mother.
He showed me people can have greatness
without any luxurious things.
His friendship is priceless.

I may be very far from you
when I walk around the landscape.
But during that trip, I'll think
about you every minute of the day.
I wish in this moment
I could be with you and no one else.
I sincerely tell you
that would've been good for my health.

Your soul will suffer
and will get despaired.
But you must be strong
because I'll wait for you everywhere.
Your heart will be sorry
you're not by my side.
But I'll never leave you.
Keep that in mind.

I'll be missing you,
thinking about your gentleness.
I'll keep loving you
with craziness.
There's no reason for you
to get insane.
You'll always know I'm alive
and your mind will not feel any pain.

I'll always be there to make your heart happy
and make your illusions come true.
Even if we're 10,000 miles apart,
I will always think about you.

You will not lose your joy.
You will miss me and I will miss you.
Even if we're very distant at this moment,
don't worry because I'll never leave you.

In that office   March 2020

I'll never forget it.
I still remember it today.
If I had any kind of joy,
that moment took it away.
My parents had to be there.
I had to see the school's dean
in that office.
I felt nervous within.

I just ended my last school year and I wanted
to enjoy that summer completely.
But something happened
and everything was ruined suddenly.
A girl, who was supposedly my friend,
said some terrible lies about me
that could've ruined me in every way.
It was something that shocked me.

I started thinking about how hard I worked
to earn that very good image.
But this person tried to hurt.
I controlled my rage.
Everything was over.
That moment was over.
I felt the anger all over me.
I thought many feelings were coming.

You can count on me   March 2020

We always told each other our things,
whether they were bad or good.
You admired me when I overcame
several obstacles, regardless of my mood.
We started talking more
and I stop being speechless.
I didn't know what to talk about sometimes,
but I started forgetting about my shyness.

There was a strange environment at the school,
but we manage to survive every time.
You dared to talk to me
and you were always kind.
If you need anything,
you can count on me.
I didn't expect our friendship to last long.
You were always friendly.

You were always there for me.
You respect the country I come from.
You never let me down.
When we talked, the sadness and anger were gone.
I'm always available
because you always treat me well.
You can count on me
if you ever need help.

Her pearls

March 2020

She starts thinking about
how she can deal with this situation.
She's afraid of starting
to feel desperation.
She thinks her beauty will start disappearing
and that brings sadness to her beautiful nature.
I can understand her pain,
but I don't know how much more I can endure.

Her tears are like pearls about to break
once they fall to the floor
and will never recover their color.
She just wants to close the door.
It's hard for me and sometimes I want to cry
because even my heart is in a sad mood
when it sees her pearl breaking like that.
She feels she will not improve.

She looks lethargic in her room,
feeling worse than a car.
She looks melancholic and uncalm.
Dealing with that inevitable sadness is hard.
That sadness will disappear, but just not now.
When she's in bed, she starts to cry.
Hey eyes start getting tired.
I want to see her sweet harmony at night.

It's hard for me because
I don't want to see her sad every day.
It's hard for me
to see her pearls break that way.

Another sister   March 2020

At the beginning, I couldn't understand her,
but as months went by,
I started knowing her
and we can even talk at night.
What she feels for me
is a clear admiration
and my personality
that doesn't have a complication.

I consider her another sister
I talk to her from home.
We clear our minds and we even talk
about what's going to come.
She talks to me about what the voices
say around the hallway.
I told her several times
I felt that same way.

She knows how the kids of my group are
and understands how I've been hurt.
She's someone impossible to hate
and one of the very few friends I have in this world.
She perfectly understands
what I've been through.
She's truly aware of how mean people can be
and what they can do.

That's why she's like another sister.
She's always been good to me.
It doesn't matter what people think.
She has great qualities people fail to see.

Self-analyze

When the teachers reprimanded them,
some boys and girls started whimpering.
They never wondered why they did it.
I don't know what they were pretending.
They were talking in class and
didn't do their work like they were supposed to.
They had to do their homework.
That's all they had to do.

They caused infernal trouble, instead of thinking
about their parents' sacrifice.
They didn't want to understand.
They had to self-analyze.
They looked like fools and thought they were
the law, never getting their act together.
There were some points of view they didn't learn.
They could've done better.

They should've been better to teachers.
Their negative legacies in that school remain.
They had to give value to the given opportunities,
but they made nonsense repeatedly.
They complicated themselves and yet,
they laughed like they were going to the mall.
Because of their lazy minds,
they made their lives harder than an iodine wall.

All those wasted opportunities will never come back
because they wanted to be too wise.
The best thing they could've done to improve
was to self-analyze.

Sad diamond

She's starting to get depressed.
She thinks how it could be possible.
She feels she'll end up losing
and the damage can be irremissible.
She thinks this will shatter her
and doesn't know what to do.
I think about pleasing her in everything,
but her sadness starts to hurt me too.

I see her in her bed
and her tears start to drop to the floor.
She feels she's declining and it's not a melodrama.
I don't know if it's a good idea to open the door.
I understand her pain and I want to relief it
because she's my most beautiful treasure.
I can't help it.
It's something hard to endure.

Her sad heart is like a diamond
that's going to break.
Her feelings are pretty and they enlighten me.
Even my soul's sad to see her diamond break that way.
Her mood will not get better today.
I comfort her when I see her cry.
I only can make hear heart feel loved
every day and night.

Her heart is so sweet and divine
and now is a lake of tears about to evaporate.
She's so special with that divine heart
that I don't want to see it deteriorate.

She feels she's dealing with torture.
I don't know if I can take it anymore.
She lays there sadly serene.
It makes me sad to see her diamond hurt.

Every event in this life
can be used as an experience.
Some may hurt, but you can learn
from them and go the distance.
Don't worry if you made the wrong move.
People can't get upset for a mistake.
If they discover their Achilles heel in one of them,
they can learn a lesson during the day.

As long as we're on the right path,
there's nothing to worry about.
If we think about weaknesses,
we can work them out.
We don't lose anything
if we know what we did wrong.
Once we analyze what the mistake was,
it's a lesson that will never be gone.

When we learn from our mistakes,
we can find out about our Achilles heel,
correct them, and learn from them.
It's a matter of self-analyzing and will.

Hurt jewel   March 2020

She starts feeling horrified
and I have never seen her like that before.
She thinks she will never heal
and when I see her like, my soul gets hurt.
I can feel that pain in her heart
that keeps affecting her.
I feel it is like a rupture,
whose noise is heard everywhere.

I see tears coming out of her eyes
and I feel her heart's starting to break
and her feelings start getting weaker.
I wish I could forget it every day.
But I admire her beautiful soul.
I see her sadness in every tearful eye.
When I see her sorrow,
I cry with her soul every night.

I would even give her a kiss in her temple
to see her face happy, but it wouldn't be fine now.
I want to cheer her up, but I'm scared of being rejected.
I want to give her comfort, but I don't know how.
It hurts me to see her in pain
and not being able to see her smile joyfully.
That pain makes her beg for clemency
and shed tears constantly.

Her soul is like a jewel that's going to break
and I don't want that to happen at any time.
It hurts me to see her hurt jewel on the ground.
I have her feelings on my mind.

Almost no one behaved
in her history class.
They caused many problems.
It didn't matter what time it was.
When they talked in class,
they caused her a big misery.
How she almost never ended
in hysteria is still a mystery.

The accumulation of disciplinary reports
in the class was inevitable.
If she made a warning, some laughed,
thinking it was fun, and that was unacceptable.
That's why she was the favorite teacher.
The warnings and reprimands kept accumulated.
She was determined to keep teaching,
but the issue escalated.

If she had to tell they had to grow up,
she told them that firmly.
She was willing to give report,
but they never took her seriously.
She was the favorite teacher
to some of my classmates.
They ignored her during class
most of the weekdays.

Favorite target   March 2020

There was a problem
if I didn't look physically good.
If I acted eccentrically, the voices
messed with me when they were in the mood.
They could not fool
because I wasn't blind.
There was always a reason
to annoy me every time.

Trying to strip me of my peace
became a daily routine.
They even teased in class, stimulating
a hate I was accumulating within.
Being the favorite target was not pretty.
It didn't matter where and when.
They would do it in different phases
and nothing could stop them.

I tried to ignore them,
but every day there was something new.
Being teased by them was like
getting a disease; it's true.
Nothing could work,
not even making a racket.
If they looked for someone to mess with,
I was their favorite target.

A hawk

I'm going on my own path,
regardless of what people can think.
I'm going against all odds
with that great determination I have within.
Even if I'm in pain,
my will to keep going will not be gone.
I want to show to the whole world
that I'm strong.

Being a hawk is an advantage because I don't
need to be in a group to have high self-esteem.
I don't need to lie because without a group,
I can go on at a great rhythm.
I feel like that bird
that uses his mind like a sword.
I keep on going with the determination of a hawk,
even though I'm alone in the world.

They hurt me several times;
they kept doing it over and over again.
They never stopped,
but I didn't get conquered by the pain.
During my school era, they gossiped
some things that were disastrous.
They thought I would end up in a world
that is lonely and thunderous.

They thought just because they underrated me,
my strong mentality would be gone.
I have a message for those who underestimated me:
You were really wrong.
I can thank you because I got stronger
when adversity gets tougher and tighter.
I don't doubt my qualities anymore.
Thanks for making me a battler.

They thought they overcame me
because they provoked every wound
with every issue I don't forget.
They thought I would lay on the ground.
They messed with me by doing several things.
I'm moving on with great determination,
acting decently, willing to face any challenge
to inspire people of a future generation.

They thought that due to their bullying,
I was going to lose my faith.
But I'm on my two feet
with my head high every day.

I want to thank them for improving my luck.
Now, I have the mentality of a fighter.
I feel I can control my destiny.
Thanks for making me a battler.

Countdown   March 2020

When I go back to my country,
I'll recover the lost time.
I will enjoy every day like a sweet melody.
I'll have that in mind.
I'll see my cousins and uncles,
whom I haven't seen in years.
They'll tell me their things, their experiences,
and what they went through; they'll be sincere.

They'll tell me their stories
and tears will be inevitable.
I'll tell them my memories
that weren't that remarkable.
They'll see how much I changed
and it's going to be sensational.
I had ups and downs, but I moved on.
The meetings will be emotional.

I'll visit every province, from Buenos Aires
to Santa Fe, if I have the chance.
I'll do it with joy,
even if I have to wander a long distance.
I'll be patient, but I'll feel great
when I step foot on the Argentine ground.
If I can work, it'll be better.
Meanwhile, I'll start the countdown.

The three wildcat girls   March 2020

Dealing with them in school
almost the whole day was horrible.
It was worse than a toothache.
Their attitude was terrible.
You had to be prepared.
They were the worst of the worst.
They could annoy you
even if you had the mentality of a warhorse.

They were mean girls
with a bad attitude and a poor mentality.
They were bullies that combined their bullying
with bad manners and rascality.
They were the bad girls
everyone loved to hate.
They were the premier example
of how a lady should not behave.

They were like headless chickens
that dared to tease anyone without a pause.
You couldn't know what trouble they were going
to provoke, always with a cause.
They got in subjects
that were none of their business.
They acted with imprudence
and they were relentless.

They were the three wildcat girls.
If you defended yourself, they complained.
But they made you lose your temper
without caring if they caused you pain.

Their constant bullying was inevitable
because they were very impulsive.
They acted like outlaws with no moral
and their behavior was repulsive.

Nothing could stop them, not even a bite
or my fists that are as solid as concrete.
They thought they were great minds, but they
were dreadful mentalities no one wanted to deal with.
They were really hated and kids
from other grades knew what they were all about.
Their bullying was so irritating
that you wanted to knock them out.

They will be remembered as troublemakers
that don't deserve honors.
They were three devils
whose bullying caused rancid odors.
How could you avoid them?
You had to figure it out
because once the three wildcat girls attacked,
there was no way out.

Bewitched   March 2020

It can be noticed
you're trying to get my attention.
I'm surprised that your actions
are not in detention.
It's clear you're bewitched with me.
I realized it's nothing weird
because you kept messing with me
every day of the year.

You think you have a rich brain, but you don't,
and you just cause stress.
You're trying to get the attention
of a boy you will never impress.
You're very delusional.
You're wasting your time.
Your bullying didn't work.
You lost your mind.

You didn't have to cause issues.
That made you earn my hate.
You just made me ignore you
and look the other way.
You almost made me lose my patience
with your constant bullying.
But you didn't have the brain
to consider my feelings.

Your bullying doesn't work, everyone knows it,
but they don't say it to you in your face.
You cause repulsion and you're
wasting your time at a great pace.

You look frustrated because you can't achieve
your goal and you don't have any ethics.
You're bewitched with me,
but your attitude is pathetic.

In the ring   March 2020

Many consider it a rough activity
because there's no thoughtfulness.
But it's something good for me
and I feel a little happiness.
I change when I get in the ring.
I can excite a little crowd.
If I get hit on the jaw,
I know the crowd will get loud.

My fists must be ready and I'm
on my own; that's part of the game.
You have to be relaxed and there's no shortcuts.
You have to tolerate pain.
When you're in the ring,
you can't show desperation.
You have a chance to go the distance.
You need to show your confidence and determination.

There're many punches to dodge
and I have a fight plan to work out.
I have to be aware in the ring
and find out what my rival is all about.
Fans get entertained, regardless of their emotions.
It's a dangerous sport,
but I like to do it and I practice it
with the heart and joy in the world.

If I'm against the ropes, I'll get a way out,
show I'm well-trained and win.
Those are the feelings I have
when I'm in the ring.

She wants to be loved   March 2020

She hears every gossip
and the details of every comment.
She doesn't want to be rejected
because she's different.
She doesn't want to accumulate wounds.
She wants that sadness of her life to be gone.
She has to locate
in a corner alone.

She wants to be loved
because she's a sensitive human being.
She wants others to be kind
and value her feelings.
She feels better when she's accepted
for being just herself.
She wants to be loved.
She's not asking for anything else.

Lost soul   March 2020

I didn't know what was happening
when I was around.
I felt I didn't fit in anywhere
and my mind was on the ground.
They saw me as a loser
and I didn't need anybody to tell me what was going on.
I remember it as an event
that was already done.

I was simply a lost soul that didn't know
very well what happened in the hallway.
I didn't need anyone to tell me
because I experienced it every day.
I didn't know what surrounded me, but I do now.
But now I can live every day and night.
I'm no longer a lost soul.
Now, I enjoy my life.

In a foreign country   March 2020

I see different structures
when I'm in a country that's not mine.
It doesn't take me long to see its good things.
I have to get used to a different time.
It's a different culture I'll never get used to.
There're different people to socialize with
and I'm not going to capitalize always.
It's something I have to deal with.

There will be people with a different
way of thinking and I don't know where to start.
They may have different genetics and ethics.
Talking to them will be hard.
When you're in a foreign country,
you'll be through big stress.
You'll miss a lot of relatives
and not everything will necessarily be the best.

I'll never forget where I come from
and a new challenge will come at a great pace.
When you're in a foreign country,
those are things you have to face.

The lonely girl   March 2020

She's in a corner alone
with nobody making her company.
People make her feel abandoned
and that happens constantly.
She feels like a drained sunflower
that's under the sun.
The lonely girl
is always on her own.

The others just ignore her.
Almost no one pays attention to her.
Nobody talks or listens to her.
It's like she's in detention.
She feels like a seagull that ends
her fly because she had a broken wing.
She feels neglected and rarely has a loyal friend,
something that makes her have a deep sadness within.

She hopes people know her like the real human being
she is, without causing a situation.
The lonely girl expects to be accepted
on some occasions.

Travelling kilometers alone   March 2020

I can see several horizons
and travel to every hemisphere.
It'll like visiting an old empire
and I could do it any given time of the year.
I'm planning to visit many streets.
I can travel kilometers alone
I want to wander around many avenues.
I can do that on my own.

Even if I don't have company,
I don't have any problem.
If I can see stadiums,
it'll be great to visit them.
If there's new radio stations
and stores to see, that's perfectly fine.
There may be hundreds of people walking,
but I'll have a great time.

I don't feel sad if I don't have company.
I have great moments when I'm on my own.
If I'm in my country, I'll feel happy
when I travel the kilometers alone.

Locked   March 2020

Those lies that girl said about me
almost ruined everything that day.
She lied about something I never did.
No one ever talked about me that way.
I wanted to be locked in my room
and not get out of there.
The embarrassment was so big
I didn't want to go anywhere.

I can't forget that hard experience.
When I slept, I had a nightmare.
My nap was clearly interrupted.
It was like I needed some air.
I asked constantly myself:
How could that happen? Why?
Nothing could comfort me.
I felt upset every night.

The suffering due to that event
was vastly deep.
It caused an internal wound
nobody should deal with.
Nobody knows how hurt
my feelings were.
During that time, I wanted to be locked
in my room and not go anywhere.

Ode to the speed bag   March 2020

When I start hitting it,
it moves forward and backwards.
It moves at a non-stop rhythm.
Working with it isn't hard.
When I use the speed bag, I'm focused
and I can't get lazy.
In the course, I got used to the noise
it makes; it doesn't drive me crazy.

Every time the bag rebounds
around, I get inspired
to train tirelessly and sweat,
even though I start getting tired.
I improve the speed in my arms
when I hit it quickly.
I did several intense three-minute rounds
when I train with it fluidly.

It's not the most complex workout,
but it makes me feel good.
When I use the speed bad, I improve my reflexes
and I get in a good mood.

A star I'll take care
of and adore   March 2020

It saddens me to see you out of nowhere
like a sad soul, completely isolated,
feeling inconsolable, with no one around you
and completely underappreciated.
You look like a little chicken coming out
of his cocoon that's abandoned
and his heart is hurt
because everyone else is gone.

You don't have to get away from me
because I want to help you heal your wounds
and recover your lost hope,
so, you don't feel doomed.
I'm being honest because your heart is
a beautiful star I don't want to see cry.
That's why I'll take care of it and adore it
every day and night.

I want to see that loving butterfly
that's beautiful on the inside
and purifies everyone's heart
with his tenderness during its flight.
Everyone has to appreciate it
because it transmits joy with passion.
I'm willing to help you heal it if
it's sad because I take it into consideration.

I'll do it with no excuses because your heart
is a beautiful star I don't want to see cry.
That's why I'll always take care of it and adore it
every day and night.

That's fine with me   March 2020

I don't need to go to jewelry shop
to get you a beautiful ring.
I just need to cheer you up,
so you can recover that joy you have within.

I can only show you
my kindness and tenderness vastly
and that can impress you.
That's fine with me.

If your sweet heart went through an event
and it just cries it
because it's broken in pieces like a bowl,
I'm willing to heal it.

You can only get love from me.
You won't get sick of it.
You feel loved and I'll feel that same way.
And that's fine with me.

Stop acting now   March 2020

I'll be honest: right now,
you look so pathetic
going to the office and playing the victim
and being hysteric.
You think I was mean when you were
the first to be inconsiderate.
Please, cut it out because I'm the one
who should be infuriated.

Don't say you feel bad
or that you're sorry because you're not.
You're sorry you couldn't take it
after you dished it out.
But you moved everyone.
It's time for you to stop the show.
You look really silly.
Stop acting now.

You go to the school's office,
thinking only about yourself.
You look like a leech blaming me
when I was just defending myself.
In the office, you say: "He started it.
I couldn't start that in any way".
I'm like: "Come on!
What other lie you're going to say?"

You start with your hurtful comments
and I defended myself without any fear.
You said I started it and it's not true.
You earned the prize of "Liar of the year".
Don't say you're sorry

because you're not.
You're sorry you couldn't take it
after you dished it out.

But you made a good drama queen scene.
It was very entertaining, but it's time to stop the show.
You entertained everyone, but it's over.
Stop acting now.

She never showed up   March 2020

We met through a social network
and we talked several times.
We agreed to see each other.
I thought everything was going to be fine.
One day, we agreed
to meet at a mall.
I kept waiting and she never showed up.
I tried to give her a call.

I called her several times,
but she never answered.
I kept waiting and waiting,
but she didn't show up anywhere.
I took it like an experience.
There was no reason to feel upset in any way.
I thought: "I'm not the only one that had
a failed meeting. There will be another day".

It was no big deal; I will have another chance.
I didn't need anyone to cheer me up.
I know nothing happened to her.
But I'll not forget the day she never showed up.

Your false apology   March 2020

Your false apology made me remember your bad action
that almost hurt my life that day.
Your false apology will not erase the negative image
I now have of you in any way.
Your false apology will not make me forget
that we were friends and you betrayed me.
Your false apology will not make me forget
the day you and your father infuriated me.
Your false apology will not forget the humiliation
my parents and I went through during that situation.
Your false apology was rejected
and I will not accept it on any occasion.

Your false remorse   March 2020

Your remorse is so false
that believing it is impossible.
Your remorse is so false
that it's laughable.
Your remorse is so false
I think it was written by a goat.
Your remorse is so false
I think you wrote an apology in a moving boat.
Your remorse is so false
nobody believed a single word.
Your remorse is so false
you couldn't convince anyone in the world.

The dawn in my soul   March 2020

When I get up, I see the dawn
and there's joy in my soul.
I see how everything will brighten up
and will form a mold.
I see a prosperous rainbow
that illuminates everything around me
so, I can walk in it
and I can see it clearly.

When I see the dawn in my soul, it feels
like a sunflower that starts blossoming
when he sees the delightful sun.
When my soul sees the daylight, the joy's never gone.
I see the birds at a branch
about singing with so much peace.
They feel very comfortable
and can share with ease.

I feel the morning will be peaceful
and my wish to live will grow.
There's no reason to feel sad.
I'll see the dawn in my soul.

Happiness in your heart   March 2020

I see happiness in your heart.
I can notice it deeply inside you.
I don't want it to vanish for any reason
because it makes me happy too.

When you show that smile everyone sees,
they see you're more beautiful than everyone thinks.
It's such a tender beauty that anyone, at any age,
can notice it and it makes everyone think.

A joy that looks like a flower
that can disappear from you, that's what I see.
Your heart's a soul so full of love
that makes a tender bird inside me.

It's a melody that creates butterflies
and it's like watching a piece of art.
That's why I will always wish
to watch the happiness in your heart.

Taking care of you until the end
is the best thing to do, so you don't feel bad.
Seeing you sad is like
seeing a nightingale sad.
I had a dream that
I saw you cornered and alone.
I wanted to make you company
so your loneliness could be gone.

Let me hear your sweet voice
that's worth hearing.
It matches your great personality.
I'll wait for you during the evening.
I'll show you love when it gets dark.
I love seeing you like a dew whose beauty I can
remember.
Come to me, sweet love.
I'll protect you from any negative force anywhere.

I'm that sweet and loving soul, a loving personality
that wants to be more than your friend.
Let me take care of your smile,
so I can take care of you until the end.

Cornered   March 2020

I see you sitting there.
Maybe you're waiting for someone.
I see you cornered and the minutes
are going by one after one.

You don't know what you're looking at,
but you're not saying a word.
You're completely quiet and I don't
if you're being delirious or you're hurt.

When I see your cornered, you're hearing
what the rest of the crowd is saying.
Maybe you're hiding a feeling because you're
isolated, while others are talking.

In the hallway

Every event happens in the hallway,
from modeling bodies gossiping everywhere
to others prying into someone else's business
because their craniums have nothing but air.

Some are hiding from someone
as they make a silly sound
and they fix their face
or they're talking, sitting on the ground.

The guys must be planning something
because they don't stop talking.
They're standing there as they
watch the modelling manicures walking.

Approach me   March 2020

I see you as a glamorous
and eternal beauty sitting there.
I feel an internal sadness when I see you like that,
being surrounded by only air.

With tears coming out of your eyes,
you're thinking you're not loved in this world
and that's the reason
you're feeling hurt.

Approach me if you have no one
to cheer you up and the sadness is still within you.
I don't want that suffering to affect
the most divine feeling inside you.

Impacted jaw   March 2020

The jaw is impacted
by several solid right hands
during a fight witnessed
by many combat fans.

You feel you got hit by a bridge
after punched by a guy who can really hit.
It's hard to take a punch by a guy
who has a punching power not many can deal with.

The rival's arms are moving, and you must hit him
because he just won't stare at you in the ring.
There's no time to get delirious.
You must face him and do your best to win.

At the shore   March 2020

I'm sitting at the shore
watching the waves getting up slowly.
Depending on the given rhythm,
they go down unexpectedly.

As the sun burns my body and I feel it,
I clear my mind.
I see many bodies having fun, playing something.
I watch how they're entertained and have a great time.

In the classroom   March 2020

In the classroom, my hand's taking notes
to pass the next test,
while the teacher of the subject is teaching,
regardless of the stress.

While a part of group population
are delirious, don't pay attention to the blackboard,
and don't listen to the authority, I listen
with all the focus in the world.

When they're not behaving correctly,
the authority loses its patience.
When they test your temper, they make you want
to lose your decency because they do it with
imprudence.

Sleepers in the classroom   March 2020

While the teachers are teaching, some
are with their eyes turned off in the classroom.
They should apply themselves and they act
like the desk is their bedroom.

The sleepers are not waking up.
Their eyes are still closed with no hesitation.
They must be dreaming because they're sleeping
like some animals in hibernation.

The teachers may show discretion,
but they know who's asleep.
Even if the nap should be interrupted,
it's an issue they deal with.

Sleeping beauties
in the classroom   March 2020

When the sleeping beauties sleep,
they gently put their heads in the desk
so, they don't have sad dreams.
It's like they want to get rid of some stress.

Once they sleep at the desk, maybe they dream
of something that can improve the relationship
they're in with their boys,
like going out on a ship.

While the teachers teach, they sleep,
something they shouldn't do.
Maybe they think in a romance and how they spend
time with their prince; that's a possibility too.

Besides the fact that they sleep,
there may be more anecdotes than this one.
Every sleeping beauty is responsible for her dream
and how they react once the class is gone.

The backboard   March 2020

When I use the backboard,
there's a bigger possibility
the ball goes in, which is what I want,
when I use it with my best ability.

When the ball goes in the net,
I feel great satisfaction.
After I used the backboard to score,
I show thirst and passion.

Using the backboard
helps a player score,
although it doesn't leave the crowd speechless
when they watch the sport.

Seeing your heart sad   March 2020

Seeing sadness in your heart in a colossal way
is like watching a fragile bowl
that just broke into many pieces.
Watching you sad is not my goal.

It's sadder than watching two seagulls
with both wings broken
that won't be able to heal
and they're frozen.

You'll hear my voice and my moves
will try to make a melody
to avoid seeing your heart sad.
I want to see in you great harmony.

At the top   March 2020

When you make it to the top,
it's a feeling you can't describe at the time.
It's a feeling you can't describe
with the best words or the best rhyme.

Those who tormented you or bullied you
because they thought they were the real deal
failed because you achieve your goals
to be at the top, by showing desire and will.

The people realized the effort you made
to get to the top is remarkable.
They see it as something great
and valuable.

The butterfly girl

I see the butterfly girl
with her dreaming soul,
her gorgeous personality,
and her charming heart wandering the world.

She's more tender than a lark.
Nobody can harm her.
No one's got anything against her.
Her personality is loved everywhere.

My heart is full of joy when he sees
the butterfly girl going everywhere
with that tenderness
her big and noble soul can offer.

Melody   March 2020

The afternoon starts getting away
and the night shows up suddenly.
Your mind is in a car
with a sadness that shows up rarely.

The silence appears only
if there's something about to be destroyed.
It only disappears
with a harmonizing joy.

I see your heart crying
and your voice starting to break.
I think how's hurting and how
I can fix it in some way.

Your heart can overcome it
with moments of love and harmony.
We can get away from all the negativity by giving
joy to every note, so we can make it a melody.

Bullying inscription

Bully, don't disturb my calm soul.
No one can stand your trouble.
You cause so many issues, it looks
you were born in a Manila jungle.

You hurt many people
and you don't care if they feel down.
Sooner or later, a person you shouldn't mess with
will knock you out in the ground.

You mess with the people, thinking
there's nothing they will dare to do.
But I can guarantee one day,
karma will catch up with you.

Operation teaching   March 2020

Teacher, be patient with my group.
I know they show their high deficiency level
and I understand it's not easy.
But not everyone is a rebel.

We depend on you
to learn the subject.
I wish all my classmates
could pay attention and show you respect.

Broken rose   March 2020

When I see a broken rose, there's an image
that appears within me suddenly.
I think of your heart, a valuable diamond that
breaks in pieces when they hurt it deeply.

I think about how it would've truly looked
had it been healthy on the grass.
But instead of looking colorful, it's
barely a shadow of what it once was.

It's a feeling that leaves your heart's
emotional state bankrupt.
When I have a broken rose in my hands,
I have that negative thought.

Violet without its petals   March 2020

Seeing a violet without its petals is like
seeing families celebrating Christmas without a tree
and without any gifts.
A person can say: "This just can't be".

It's like seeing the last of that beauty
that gives signs of life to your heart and your mind
and all of a sudden, they hurt it
and finish it in just a matter of time.

A violet without its petal is a sad image
of a beautiful maiden's personality
interrupted by a hurting force
that wounded her deeply.

A riot   March 2020

There are hundreds of bodies
on their seats watching.
Then, they're standing up
and they start protesting.

Scandal starts breaking out
and objects are being thrown.
They all are looking like vandals after starting a mess
and others don't know when it'll be gone.

Sometimes people start hearing
a rough thundering sound.
They act like animals and it's not normal.
That happens when a riot starts breaking down.

Girl of the devil   March 2020

Her nasty behavior makes her
earn the hate of many easily.
When people hear her voice, they hear
every word that can hurt deeply.

It's as bad as damaging earth with nitroglycerine.
Hearing her is prejudicial for our brain.
Nobody can stop the girl of the devil.
She's worse than a hurricane.

Not even the authority can stop her.
The girl of the devil is incorrigible.
She's an annoying bully.
She's extremely terrible.

Abandoned guitar

March 2020

It's still alive, well kept in a black bag
I have it there despite it's out of tune.
The guitar hasn't been used in a long time.
I know I can use it soon.
I never forgot about that instrument
that helped me deal with stress.
Those times when I practiced
with it were truly the best.

I felt very relaxed
when I used to play it.
I can remember those good times with the guitar.
It's impossible to forget it.

Eager guitar   March 2020

The guitar has a big desire
to be in tune and used again.
It's nothing new if a person
plays it, he can be entertained.

She wants a song to be played
with a lot of musicality.
It must captivate others' attention,
although it doesn't need to have fragility.

She doesn't want to see a sad, depressed girl.
She wants a melody to be played,
so she can feel better and improve
people's adrenaline during the day.

Although they're not used with the best aim,
millions are sold in a dishonest way.
But when they get to the wanted destination,
they can cause a hole in you any given day.

When the projectiles impact,
they do it in any part available.
Once they do it, the damage they cause
can be irreversible.

The impacted body feels it
and goes to the ground slowly.
It doesn't matter if other souls are hurt.
They can end a life permanently.

.

Determined hawk   March 2020

He doesn't care if a meteor
comes at a really high speed.
He'll try to pass it,
so everyone remembers his myth.

He's normally alone.
No one makes him company.
When he travels miles,
he does it incessantly.

He shows he's a determined hawk
every time he flies in the air.
He keeps flying with desire and determination.
Without company, he can go anywhere.

Fists flying   March 2020

The crowd is staying alert
when the fists are flying.
When they fly, they know the path,
but they don't land at the destination they're wishing.

The crowd is waiting for a left
hand or a right hand to land.
Suddenly, they get excited
with the knockdown of either man.

Once the fists are landing
on the target wanted,
the crowd gets more excited,
making a big racket.

Beauty without a mentality   March 2020

You think you have greatness because you attract
others with your beauty to your center.
But when someone inspects your cranium,
there's nothing there and that doesn't even attract the
weather.

Yes, I can see there's a great figure
that can clearly attract someone anywhere.
There may be something beautiful,
but the mentality's not necessarily there.

To impress someone, you need more than beauty.
You have to be smart.
Trying to attract someone by just being
a pretty girl is extremely hard.

You may have a body that attracts
guys with vulnerability.
But you really showed
that you're a beauty without a mentality.

Abandoned puppy   March 2020

When I see an abandoned puppy,
I think in a sweet lost soul
who was left on his own
and doesn't have anyone in the world.

They leave him alone, with nobody
to make him company; he's really alone.
He thinks: "What did I do to make them
leave me this way?". This just began.

If he gets other dogs to make him company,
he feels a little better, but his life's still hard.
The day he's helped and loved,
it'll bring a big joy to his heart.

General bully

He always has his pack,
with his same mentality, making him company.
When you see their faces, you can notice
their brain activity wasn't developed properly.

He leads everything,
whether he's alone or with his gang.
He looks for trouble, even in a road walk.
He thinks he's acting like a man.

When he's with his gang,
he knows one thing: causing pure terror.
For others who have to stand him for months,
it's something that provokes horror.

The general bully always looks for a victim
to make him lose his serenity.
With or without his gang, he torments people tirelessly
and try to get away with it with vast impunity.

The truck driver   March 2020

The truck driver travels thousands of kilometers
using any kind of shortcut.
He ends up driving to many places
to do his job.

He's always seated
with his hands on the steering wheel.
He must be focused
to avoid losing control of his wheels.

He takes any direction to go his destiny,
regardless of the weather; it's a big sacrifice.
He rarely has company and his job
is one nobody can criticize.

My Argentine flag   March 2020

I have the colors blue, yellow, and sky-blue
in my heart and I'll defend them like a man.
Although I live in another country,
I'll love it until the end.

When I see that beautiful face in the center,
centered by the yellow sun,
it makes me love my country more.
I don't forget where I come from.

The love for my flag is huge.
I always treat it with consideration.
It's a divine feeling I have
because it represents my nation.